Birds of Guyana

Birds of Guyana

Balram Singh

MACMILLAN
CARIBBEAN

Macmillan Education
Between Towns Road, Oxford OX4 3PP
A division of Macmillan Publishers Limited
Companies and representatives throughout the world

www.macmillan-caribbean.com

ISBN 0 333 97557 X

Text © Balram Singh 2004
Design and illustration © Macmillan Publishers Limited 2004

First published 2004

All rights reserved; no part of this publication may be reproduced, stored in a retrieval system, transmitted in any form or by any means, electronic, mechanical, photocopying, recording, or otherwise, without the prior written permission of the publishers.

Typeset by CjB Editorial Plus
Illustrated by TechType
Cover design by Gary Fielder, AC Design
Cover photograph by Robert J. Fernandes

Printed and bound in Malaysia

2008 2007 2006 2005 2004
10 9 8 7 6 5 4 3 2 1

Contents

Preface	vi
Map of Guyana	vii
Introduction	viii
1 The Hoatzin	1
2 Birds of prey	3
3 Waders and waterbirds	15
4 Insect eaters	33
5 Grain and seed eaters	53
6 Fruit eaters	65
Index	88

Preface

Birds of Guyana is another volume in the highly successful Macmillan Caribbean Pocket Natural History Series. Guyana is the only English-speaking country in South America, and for the first time the series affords us a glimpse of the fascinating birds of this continent.

Guyana is particularly blessed with an abundance of bird life, with over 780 species recorded as compared with only 560 species for the whole of Europe. The expanded edition of *Birds of Guyana* features 80 species recorded in remote locations of the interior as well as in the coastal lowlands.

The text for this book was provided by Mr Balram Singh, zoologist, ornithologist and taxidermist, who is a leading authority on the birds of Guyana. With 39 years' experience at the National Museum and Zoo, he has travelled extensively in the interior of Guyana on field trips, to study and collect a wide range of local birds. Balram Singh is retired and now lives in Toronto, Canada, where he is always willing to share his knowledge of the fauna of Guyana.

All photographs were taken by Robert J. Fernandes unless otherwise indicated below. He is Guyana's foremost nature photographer, and has published several books featuring the natural beauty of his homeland.

Boat-Billed Heron: Peter Fernandes DVM
Jabiru Stork, Black Skimmer, Vermilion Flycatcher, Fork-tailed Flycatcher, Paradise Jacamar, Little Chachalaca: Patrick DeGroot

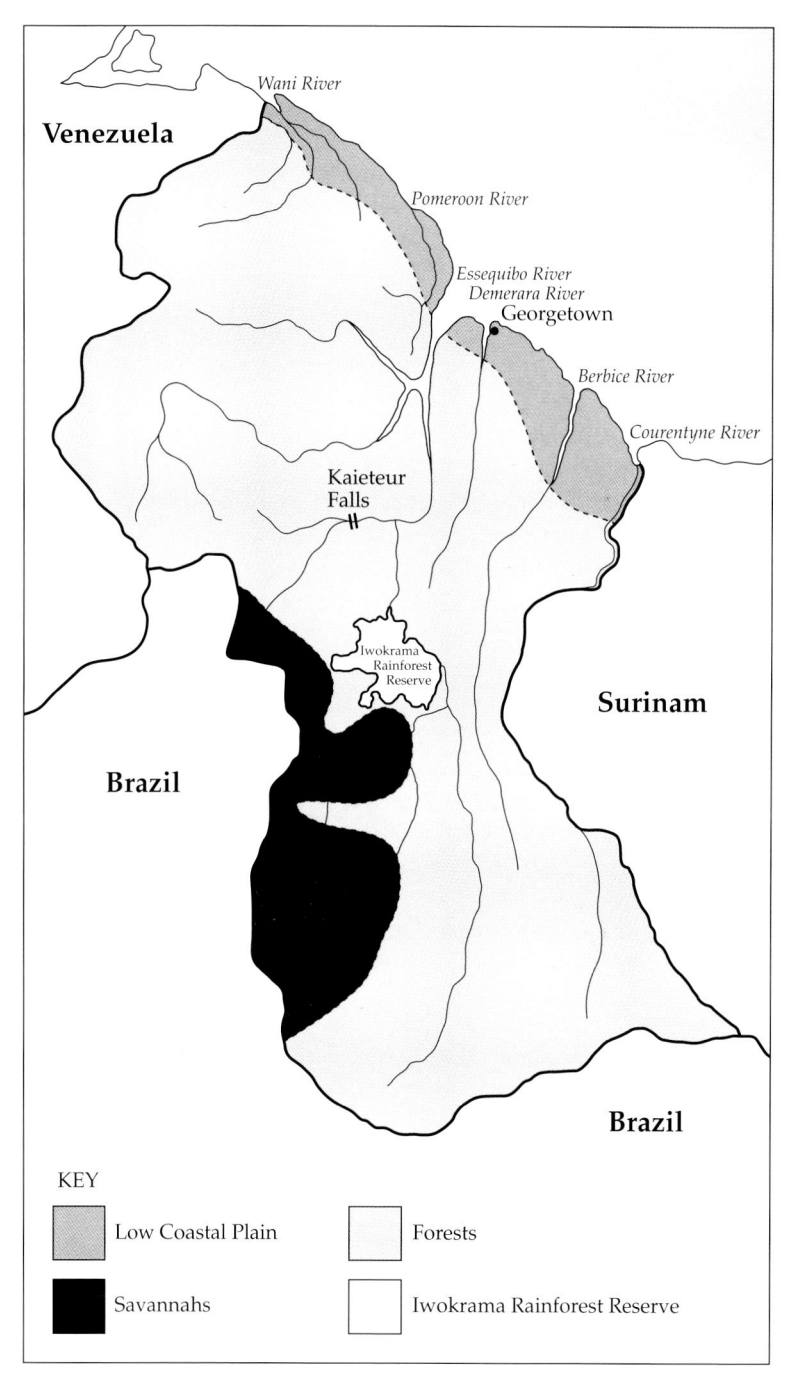

Map of Guyana showing habitats

Introduction

With its three distinct natural regions, Guyana boasts such vast and varied habitats that it is able to sustain a remarkably diverse range of birds. Geographically it is part of the great Amazon River basin: approximately three quarters of its 215,000 km^2 (83,000 sq miles) are covered with tropical rainforest, and as a result it shares the bird life of this region.

In stark contrast to the rainforest, vast tracts of grassland known as the Rupununi Savannahs cover the south-western corner of Guyana. This is a delicate ecosystem, complete with many indigenous species of birds.

Guyana has over 300 km (200 miles) of Atlantic coastlands. These lowlands are home to 90 per cent of the country's population and a great number of species. Habitats include large river estuaries, coastal mangrove, fresh-water marshlands and extensive plantations of rice and sugar. The birds of this region literally overflow into the towns and villages along the coast.

For the purpose of simplification this book has been divided into chapters, one for each basic group of birds. These include birds of prey, waders and waterbirds, insect eaters, grain and seed eaters, and fruit eaters. Although these families have many different characteristics, one of the easiest ways of identifying them is by their beaks.

The different groups of birds

The **Hoatzin**, which is the national bird of Guyana, is ornithologically in a class by itself, and it has therefore been treated separately.

Birds of prey, or flesh eaters, are birds whose diet consists either of live animals or of the rotting carcasses of dead animals. These birds have large, strong talons, which they use to seize and hold their prey so that they can tear it with their sharp, heavily hooked beaks as they feed. This group includes eagles, hawks, vultures and owls.

Birds of prey

Waders and waterbirds are usually slender birds with long, sharp, dagger-like beaks. They are aquatic feeders, and can venture into the water on stilt-like legs in order to spear fish, crabs and frogs. This group includes herons, egrets, sandpipers and plovers.

Insect eaters are a large, varied and common group of birds. They have broad, flattened beaks, which are slightly hooked at the end, and tufts of hair or bristles at the base of the beak, where it joins the head. They are skilful fliers, as most of the insects on which they feed must be caught on the wing. Members of this family include kiskadees, swallows and wrens.

Waders

Insect eaters

INTRODUCTION ix

Grain and seed eaters

Grain and seed eaters are a large group of small birds. They have short, stubby beaks that look heavy for their size. These beaks are specially designed for grinding the small grass seeds that make up their diet. Another way to identify this group of birds is by their wide range of melodious whistles and calls, as they include all birds referred to locally as 'cage birds', such as Finches and Canaries.

Fruit eaters are also a widespread and varied group of birds. Their beaks are usually not long, but are conical and slightly curved in shape. However, the group also includes parrots and toucans, which have specialised beaks. Parrots and macaws have strong, sharply hooked beaks that can crack the seeds and nuts that, along with fruit, make up their diet. The exact function of the toucan's spectacularly large bill is still a mystery, as its main diet consists of soft fruits, although it occasionally robs nests to feed on young birds and eggs. Other members of this family include Tanagers and Orioles.

Fruit eaters

Feeding

Different types of bird vary widely in their choices of food. They include flesh, fish, crabs, reptiles, carrion, eggs, worms, fruit, nectar, insects, seeds, grain and even leaves. So quite a large population of different species can be found inhabiting a small area of the countryside. Nocturnal species – birds that are active at night – also have access to different types of food from that available to daytime feeders.

Some birds are beneficial to their habitats: for example, owls help keep their surroundings free from rats, mice and even harmful snakes. Insect eaters are the farmer's friend, as they help to control the harmful insects that affect the crops. Vultures provide an important service by disposing of the decaying bodies of animals and other carrion.

However, there are also some species of birds that are considered pests. For example, Black-bellied Whistling Ducks are the enemy of the rice farmer, as they descend on the rice fields in large flocks to feed on the freshly sown paddy. In the forests of the interior, the farms are plagued by flocks of macaws and parrots, which do considerable damage to corn and other fruit crops. In both cases hunting is used to control the numbers of birds.

Nesting

If you see a bird with a piece of strange material in its beak it is a sure sign that nesting time has arrived. Birds' nests vary in size from that of the Hummingbird, which may be only 5 cm (2 inches) in diameter, to the nest of the Harpy Eagle, which can measure 2 m (6 feet) across. Nests come in an endless array of designs. Some are unbelievable works of skill, delicately braided from all kinds of plant fibres, feathers, animal hair and spider web. Others, such as those of the larger birds of prey, are just untidy collections of sticks laid out on the flat surface of a branch. Some birds simply use existing holes in tree-trunks or crevices in rocks with no nesting material at all. To evade predators, birds usually locate their nests in sheltered places: sometimes concealed in caves or thick thorn bushes, sometimes high in the treetops or suspended from the outermost branches of tall trees.

Tinamou nest

Birds' nests have been found in the strangest places: around houses, in letterboxes, on bookshelves, in old shoes and even in the guard of a traffic light completely blocking out the green light. Not every bird builds a nest; some lay their eggs along with others of their own species in one big communal nest, whereas others simply eject the rightful owners of the nest once they have finished building it. However, probably the most amazing nest behaviour is that of birds that simply lay their eggs in the nests of other birds, leaving the young to be reared entirely by their foster parents. Because of this you may come across the strange sight of a small parent feeding a nestling twice its size.

Plumage

The colours of some birds can be misleading. Once they leave the nest, many young birds are indistinguishable from their parents, but others are the complete opposite, having such vastly different colours and markings from the adult that they are often mistaken for an entirely different species. Two of the most striking examples of this are the Wattled Jacana chick and immature Night Heron. This stage of contrasting coloration can last for up to a year, and during this time the young birds are known as **juveniles**.

Night Heron and young

The main reason for this difference in plumage is that it serves as a form of camouflage to protect the young birds from predators. Although many birds seem spectacularly coloured when they are separated from their natural habitat – for example a parrot when seen in a cage – the same bird, observed in its natural surroundings, can sometimes seem to 'disappear' right before your eyes. A motionless parrot between leaves is extremely difficult to detect even from a few metres away.

Camouflaged parrot

Bird calls

In the wild the songs and calls of birds are valuable in identifying some species. In fact we are usually not aware that birds are close by until we hear their whistles or calls. As well as their usual song, birds make a variety of other sounds, such as alarm calls, mating calls, parental calls and even special calls while in flight. Each of these calls is distinctly different and has an important function in the bird's life. Many otherwise drab and unattractive birds, such as the Thrush and the Wren, have the most musical whistles and songs. Through the ages the sweet melodious songs of birds have been so treasured that they have been kept in cages purely for people's enjoyment.

Birds of Guyana will be of interest and assistance to the casual birdwatcher and ornithologist alike. It is the author's wish that it will not only encourage bird-watching enthusiasts to visit Guyana, but may also inspire the publication of a more comprehensive and scientific volume on Guyana's truly amazing bird life.

Some useful references

The Birds of Guyana, Formerly British Guiana: A Checklist of 720 Species. Dorothy Snyder. 1966, Peabody Museum, Salem, Massachusetts.

Birds of Surinam, 2nd edition. F. Haverschmidt and G.F. Mees. 1994, VACO, Paramaribo, Surinam.

Birds of Venezuela. Steven L. Hilty. 2003, Christopher Helm, London.

A Field Checklist of the Birds of Guyana. Michael J. Braun, Davis W. Finch, Mark B. Robbins and Brian K. Schmidt. 2000, Smithsonian Institution, Washington, DC.

1 The Hoatzin

Hoatzin (*Opisthocomus hoazin*)

Hoatzin
Opisthocomus hoazin

Local name: Canje Pheasant
Family: Hoatzin

Distribution

The Hoatzin is Guyana's national bird. Pheasant-like in appearance, its amazing physical characteristics make it unique in the world of birds.

Famous naturalist and explorer William Beebe, after visiting Guyana, wrote: 'The Hoatzin is a strange reptile-like bird, a living fossil which is related to no other living bird and can only be found in this part of the world.'

The Hoatzin's extremely limited habitat is the thick vegetation on the banks of the Mahaica, Mahaicony, Abary and Canje creeks, including the Berbice River. In the past it has also been recorded in the Takatu River. Its food consists solely of the leaves and fruit of the Muca-Muca, Bunduri and Courida plants that make up its tangled habitat. As a result of this restricted diet, the Hoatzin cannot be kept in captivity.

A weak flier, the Hoatzin is usually seen climbing clumsily about in the riverbank undergrowth. However, it is the nestlings that exhibit the most remarkable characteristics. The young birds have a claw at the bend of each wing that they use to climb about in the vegetation soon after birth. If danger threatens, the almost naked chick will let itself fall into the water, where it can swim and dive skilfully, only to claw its way back into the undergrowth when it is safe to do so.

The Hoatzin is known locally as the Canje Pheasant or 'Stinking Hannah' because the bird gives off a strong musky odour, resembling that of fresh cow dung. One theory is that this strange smell is caused by the half-digested leaves in the bird's stomach.

The nest is a collection of loosely arranged twigs, usually located overhanging water. The range of the Hoatzin is extremely limited: the bird occurs only in small areas of the northern countries of South America, including the Guianas, Venezuela, Columbia, Brazil and Ecuador.

Hoatzin chicks

2 Birds of prey

King Vulture (*Sarcoramphus papa*)

Harpy Eagle
Harpia harpyja

Family: Hawks and Eagles

Distribution

Harpy Eagle (*Harpia harpyja*)

The Harpy Eagle is the largest eagle in the world. Over 1 m (3 feet) high, with a wingspan of up to 2 m (6 feet), it can weigh between 7.3 and 7.7 kg (16–17 lb). The female of the species is larger than the male. The Harpy inhabits the densely forested areas of the interior and the forest bordering the Rupununi Savannahs. A hunter adapted for moving in dense vegetation, it feeds on monkeys, sloths and large birds, which it pursues aggressively through the treetops. Even on the forest floor it can catch Agoutis, Pacas and Armadillos with great agility. It is difficult to imagine any other bird of prey competing with the Harpy as it hunts by day in the forest. The nest, more than 2 m (6 feet) in diameter, is constructed of large twigs and branches, usually found in the tallest trees 15–20 m (50–60 feet) from the ground. The Harpy Eagle is only found in the Western Hemisphere, where it ranges from Central America in the north through South America to Argentina in the south.

Crested Caracara

Caracara cheriway

Family: Falcons and Caracaras

Distribution

The Crested Caracara is one of the most colourful birds of prey. It inhabits the savannahs of the interior as well as the mangroves and open country of the coastlands, where it is quite common. This bird is generally social in habits, and can be seen in pairs or large groups of 20 or more in freshly ploughed fields. Unlike other members of the falcon family that are great fliers, this rather sluggish bird spends most of its time on the ground, where it can sometimes be seen running swiftly to catch insects, small rodents or reptiles. The Caracara is also a scavenger and will often compete with vultures to feed on a carcass. The nest is a bulky, bowl-like construction of twigs and sticks located in trees. The Crested Caracara ranges from the southern USA down through most of Central and South America.

Crested Caracara (*Caracara cheriway*)

Snail Kite
Rostrhamus sociabilis

Local name: Chicken Hawk or Kreketty Hawk
Family: Kites, Hawks and Eagles

Distribution

Quite common in coastal regions, the Snail Kite prefers wet marshy areas such as swamps, mangroves, rice fields and the trenches that border them. In these habitats the snails that are its main diet can easily be found. The feeding ritual of this hawk is fascinating to watch. It can often be seen flying slowly over the water until a snail is located below. It then hovers lightly and drops almost gently with claws outstretched to pluck its prey from the water and fly off to feed. Its strong hooked beak is specially adapted for extracting the snail from its shell. The bird's favourite fence post perch can be easily identified by the hundreds of empty shells that accumulate there. Birds, lizards and snakes are also eaten. The Snail Kite nests in groups, making a rough platform of twigs in low trees and shrubbery. It ranges from Florida in the north through Central and South America as far south as Argentina.

Snail Kite (*Rostrhamus sociabilis*)

White-tailed Hawk *Buteo albicaudatus*

Local name: Chicken Hawk
Family: Kites, Hawks and Eagles

Distribution

White-tailed Hawk (*Buteo albicaudatus*)

The White-tailed Hawk is one of the more common hawks in Guyana. Widespread along the forest edges of both the coastland and the interior, it is also found in the coconut plantations and the open grasslands. A screaming cry often causes it to be seen on the uppermost branches of the trees in its habitat, where it is an active hunter by day. Its varied prey consists of small mammals, birds, lizards, snakes and insects. The nest is a rough platform of sticks in trees or other dense foliage. The White-tailed Hawk ranges from Trinidad through the countries of northern South America, as far south as Argentina.

BIRDS OF PREY

Ornate Hawk-Eagle *Spizaetus ornatus*

Family: Kites, Hawks and Eagles Distribution

Ornate Hawk-Eagle (*Spizaetus ornatus*)

This colourful raptor is uncommon and is seldom seen, as it inhabits the lowland and mountain forests of the interior. It is usually found in pairs soaring high above its habitat, where it sometimes performs diving displays accompanied by high-pitched screaming calls. Its diet consists of birds, both in flight and from the forest, as well as Agouti, Paca and smaller forest animals. A fairly large nest of sticks lined with leaves and grass is made in the forks of high trees. The range of the Ornate Hawk-Eagle extends from Mexico to Trinidad and most of the countries of South America.

Black and White Hawk-Eagle *Spizastur melanoleucus*

Family: Kites, Hawks and Eagles

Distribution

Black and White Hawk-Eagle (*Spizastur melanoleucus*)

With its contrasting plumage, the Black and White Hawk-Eagle is one of the most beautiful birds of prey found in Guyana. This solitary, uncommon bird can sometimes be seen soaring over the more remote forests of the interior, which are its habitat. Its prey consists of large birds such as the Curassow and Guan, as well as the small mammals and reptiles found in the forest. It usually nests in high trees, where it constructs an untidy platform of sticks. The Black and White Hawk-Eagle ranges from Mexico in the north, through Central and South America, as far south as Argentina.

Bat Falcon

Falco rufigularis

Local name: Baridi Hawk
Family: Falcons and Caracaras

Distribution

Noted for its incredible speed of flight, the Bat Falcon is one of the fastest birds in the world. Fairly common in the open country of the coastlands, this fierce hunter can also be found in the more remote forests of the interior. Soaring above the countryside it uses its keen eyesight to locate its prey, and then – diving at speeds estimated to reach in excess of 100 km/hr (60 mph) – it seizes the unsuspecting bird in mid-air and returns to its perch to feed. Its prey includes bats, parrots, pigeons, swallows and insects. It generally uses the nests of other birds in the holes of trees. The Bat Falcon ranges from Mexico in the north, through Central America, Trinidad, Venezuela, Surinam, Peru and Bolivia, as far south as Argentina.

Bat Falcon (*Falco rufigularis*)

10   BIRDS OF GUYANA

Spectacled Owl

Pulsatrix perspicillata

Family: Owls

Distribution

The Spectacled Owl gets its name from its white face markings, which encircle its eyes like spectacles. This uncommon bird has a wide range of habitats including coastal mangroves, savannahs and forests of the interior. Not strictly nocturnal, it can be seen in broad daylight, alone or in pairs. As for all members of the owl family, the extraordinary softness of its plumage makes its flight completely noiseless. This is useful when hunting its prey, which consists of rats, lizards, frogs, small birds and insects. The Spectacled Owl nests in holes in trees, and ranges from Mexico, through South America, as far south as Argentina.

Spectacled Owl (*Pulsatrix perspicillata*)

Great Horned Owl

Bubo virginianus

Family: Owls

Distribution

Great Horned Owl
(*Bubo virginianus*)

The Great Horned Owl is the largest species of owl to be found in Guyana. Its name is derived from its most prominent feature: two large tufts of feathers, resembling horns, on the top of its head. Generally found alone or in pairs, it prefers to hunt on the borders of the forest, river banks, swamps and coastal mangroves. In these habitats it is not uncommon. Not entirely nocturnal, it uses its mottled brown plumage as a daytime camouflage against other birds that disturb it. The Great Horned Owl has a wide range of prey, consisting of mice, rats, bats, reptiles, birds and mammals. It is therefore useful as a pest exterminator. Old abandoned nests of big birds of prey as well as burrows are used for breeding. The Great Horned Owl ranges throughout most of North, Central and South America, from Alaska to Argentina.

Black Vulture   *Coragyps atratus*

Local name: Carrion Crow
Family: New World Vultures

Distribution

Black Vulture (*Coragyps atratus*)

The Black Vulture is the most common and conspicuous of the four species of vulture found in Guyana. It frequents the open country around coastal and interior settlements, especially around slaughterhouses. It feeds almost exclusively by scavenging, and can be seen singly or in flocks soaring at great heights above the countryside, where it uses its keen eyesight to identify rotting carcasses or other carrion. Its rough, unlined nest can be found on the ground, between rocks, thick foliage and hollow logs. The Black Vulture ranges from the USA through Central and South America.

King Vulture — *Sarcoramphus papa*

Family: New World Vultures   Distribution

King Vulture
(*Sarcoramphus papa*)

The King Vulture is by far the largest and most beautiful of the four species of vulture found in Guyana. This uncommon bird occurs in the forested areas of the interior and the open country of the Great Savannahs and hilly regions. With a wingspan of 2 m (6.5 feet), it is usually seen soaring high in the air, either alone or with other species of vulture, although it remains aloof and on the edge of the flock. It is mainly a scavenger, feeding on the carcasses of dead animals and other carrion. When it makes its appearance at a feeding site, other vultures retreat to a safe distance until the larger bird has finished feeding. Surprisingly, this great rider of the air currents builds its nest either on the ground or close to it, in old logs and tree stumps. The King Vulture ranges from Mexico in the north through Central and South America to Argentina in the south.

3 Waders and waterbirds

Tricolored Heron (*Egretta tricolor*)

Cattle Egret
Bubulcus ibis

Local name: Gauling
Family: Herons

Distribution

First recorded in British Guiana in 1937, the Cattle Egret is an African migrant species that has established itself so well in Guyana that it is now one of our most common birds. It can easily be distinguished from the other White Egrets by its yellow beak and the light brown feathers of its mating plumage. It follows cattle, sheep and other grazing animals, picking the ticks off them and feeding on the grasshoppers and other insects that they disturb in the grass. Not shy, the bird frequents residential areas, and can be seen at the side of roads, where it also catches lizards and frogs as well as the insects that make up its main diet. Unlike the other species of egret it does not spend much time near water, but can be seen in great flocks following the tractors as they plough the rice fields. The Cattle Egret is so numerous that it is seriously challenging the other indigenous species of egrets for nesting sites that are usually just platforms of twigs placed on horizontal branches. It ranges throughout most of the Western Hemisphere, as well as Europe, Africa, Asia and Australia.

Cattle Egret (*Bubulcus ibis*)

Great Egret — *Ardea alba*

Local name: White Crane
Family: Herons

Distribution

Great Egret (*Ardea alba*)

The Great Egret is the largest of all the species of egret found in Guyana. It is common in the coastal mud-flats and estuaries, as well as the waterways of the interior savannahs. Its diet consists of fish, crabs, frogs, lizards and snakes. It nests in mixed colonies along with other egrets and herons. The nest of the Great Egret is an untidy platform of sticks usually found in trees or low brush. In addition to the Western Hemisphere, this bird is also found in Europe, Africa, Asia and Australia.

Cocoi Heron
Ardea cocoi

Local name: Honorora Crane
Family: Herons

Distribution

The Cocoi Heron, approximately 1.2 m (4 feet) in height, is the largest of the many species of heron that occur in Guyana. This somewhat shy, solitary bird is fairly common in coastal mudflats, swamps, rice fields, and along the inland waterways. Apart from fish, frogs, crabs and other forms of aquatic life, it also eats snakes and young birds. When feeding, it walks with slow methodical movements in shallow water and then, with a sudden darting thrust, expertly spears its prey with its long sharp bill. When disturbed, this graceful bird with its large wingspan appears to fly in slow motion, only to settle 50 or so metres away to continue foraging. The nest is a collection of sticks, roughly put together high up in bushes close to water. The Cocoi Heron ranges from Panama and Trinidad through most of South America.

Cocoi Heron (*Ardea cocoi*)

Striated Heron *Butorides striatus*

Local name: Chow
Family: Herons

Distribution

The Striated Heron, one of the smaller species of heron, is widespread among the marshes and waterways of both the coastlands and the interior. It can be commonly seen near towns and other settlements, flicking its short tail, as it forages for fish, frogs, lizards and insects. Its nest is a platform of twigs lined with vegetation, which is usually away from the water, in low shrubs or mangroves. It is found not only in Trinidad and most of the countries of South America, but also in Africa and Australia.

Striated Heron (*Butorides striatus*)

Tricolored Heron

Egretta tricolor

Local name: Gauling
Family: Herons

Distribution

Tricolored Heron (*Egretta tricolor*)

This graceful, medium-sized heron is a solitary bird that can often be seen close to human settlements. It is found throughout the coastal mud-flats, mangroves and freshwater marshes, where it can be seen patiently contemplating the shallows for its prey. Its diet consists of fish, crabs, shrimp, frogs and insects, which are abundant in its habitat. It nests in mixed colonies of Herons and Egrets in mangrove and other waterside vegetation, where it constructs an untidy platform of sticks. The Tricolored Heron ranges from the USA, through the West Indies and the northern countries of South America, as far south as Brazil.

Black-crowned Night Heron — *Nycticorax nycticorax*

Local name: Quack
Family: Herons

Distribution

Black-crowned Night Heron (*Nycticorax nycticorax*)

The Black-crowned Night Heron is the only heron in Guyana that is mainly nocturnal. It passes the daylight hours in hunched sleeping positions, concealed in the thick shrubbery and mangroves bordering salt and freshwater marshes. At dusk its hoarse 'quacking' calls can be heard as it flies from its daytime roost in large flocks to the tidal mud-flats along the seashore. Here it feeds throughout the night on a wide variety of fish and other aquatic life. This heron nests in large flocks, often in the company of other herons and egrets. The nest is a loosely arranged platform of twigs on the branches of trees. The Black-crowned Night Heron is almost worldwide in distribution, as it occurs not only in the Western Hemisphere but also in Europe and Asia.

Boat-billed Heron *Cochlearius cochlearius*

Local name: Crapaud Quack
Family: Herons

Distribution

Boat-billed Heron (*Cochlearius cochlearius*)

The Boat-billed Heron is readily identifiable from the other species of the heron family by its wide bill and large eyes, which indicate some nocturnal activity. It is a solitary bird that, although widespread, is hard to see in the mangrove swamps and the dense undergrowth along the banks of inland rivers that are its habitat. Its diet consists of shrimp, crabs, fish, frogs, lizards and insects. This heron nests among the thick shrubbery and reeds by the water edge, where it lays out an untidy platform of sticks. It can be found in Mexico, Trinidad and most South American countries.

Rufescent Tiger-Heron *Tigrisoma lineatum*

Local name: Tiger Bird
Family: Herons

Distribution

Rufescent Tiger-Heron (*Tigrisoma lineatum*)

This heron is a solitary bird, widespread in the tangled vegetation along the creeks and rivers of both the coastland and the interior. A master of camouflage, it has striped plumage that blends with the vegetation of its habitat. If it is in danger, it will remain motionless or sway gently with the movement of the surrounding vegetation. Its diet consists of fish, frogs, snails, crustaceans, worms and insects. The nest is an untidy platform of marsh vegetation in the dense shrubs. The Rufescent Tiger-Heron ranges from Trinidad, through most of South America, to Argentina in the south.

Maguari Stork *Euxenura maguari*

Local name: Heeri
Family: Storks

Distribution

Maguari Stork (*Euxenura maguari*)

The Maguari Stork is one of Guyana's larger marsh birds. It occurs in moderate groups along the coastal rivers and water conservancies, as well as the wetlands of the Rupununi Savannahs, where it is often seen circling overhead. Like other waders, its diet consists of fish, frogs, toads and snakes found near the water's edge. With its great bill it can even feed on some of the larger species, which it swallows whole with a backward toss of its head. Its nest is a collection of sticks put together in the fork of a large tree. It ranges throughout the continent of South America, as far south as Argentina and Chile.

Jabiru Stork
Jabiru mycteria

Local name: Negrocop
Family: Storks

Distribution

The Jabiru is the tallest if not the largest bird in Guyana, and is widely distributed throughout the wetlands of the coast as well as the savannahs of the interior. With a wingspan of over 2 m (6 feet), it can be easily identified circling high above the rice fields and marshlands that make up its habitat. It is entirely carnivorous, feeding on the larger species of fish, frogs, crustaceans and reptiles. A solitary bird, its nest consists of a large platform of sticks, usually in the forks of high trees. It ranges from Mexico, through Central and South America, as far south as Argentina.

Jabiru Stork (*Jabiru mycteria*)

WADERS AND WATERBIRDS 25

Limpkin

Aramus guarauna

Local name: Karow
Family: Limpkins

Distribution

The Limpkin is a solitary bird that can be seen foraging, with an odd limping gait, in the rice fields and marshlands of the coast. Although it is a good swimmer it prefers shallow water, where it feeds mainly on snails, but will also include frogs, lizards and insects in its diet. It builds a flimsy, shallow nest of sticks and vegetation in a secluded spot near the water or in low shrubbery. It ranges from the USA through Central America, most of the Caribbean and South America, as far south as Argentina.

Limpkin (*Aramus guarauna*)

Southern Lapwing

Vanellus chilensis

Family: Plovers

Distribution

A handsome bird, the Southern Lapwing is difficult to see on the ground, but is conspicuous in flight, especially by its unmistakable alarm call. Often seen in large flocks, it is common in the coastal grasslands, rice fields and the savannahs of the interior. It forages by day and by night, running quickly along the ground in search of snails, beetles, lizards and frogs. Its nest is an unlined shallow hollow in the ground of the open grassland of its habitat. Its range includes Panama, Colombia, Venezuela, Brazil, as far south as Chile.

Southern Lapwing (*Vanellus chilensis*)

WADERS AND WATERBIRDS

Black-bellied Whistling-Duck — *Dendrocygna autumnalis*

Local name: Wissy-Wissy
Family: Ducks

White-faced Whistling-Duck — *Dendrocygna viduata*

Family: Ducks

Distribution

The Black-bellied and White-faced Whistling-Ducks are the most common of the three species of whistling-duck recorded in Guyana. They share the same habitats along coastal rivers, savannah marshes and rice fields. Partially active at night, they feed on fish, frogs and aquatic insects. They also have a special preference for paddy, and can do considerable damage to rice crops, which is why they are considered a pest by farmers. As a result, the shooting of these birds has greatly reduced their numbers along the coastlands. These species all have whistling calls. They nest in holes in trees or between reeds and bushes by the water's edge; the nests are usually shared by more than one female. The Black-bellied ranges further north from Texas and is joined by the White-faced through Central and South America as far as northern Argentina.

Black-bellied Whistling-Duck (*Dendrocygna autumnalis*) and White-faced Whistling-Duck (*Dendrocygna viduata*)

Spotted Sandpiper

Actitis macularia

Local name: Shakey
Family: Sandpipers

Distribution

The Spotted Sandpiper is one of the most common migrants, but is not as numerous as the other small shorebirds. Seen throughout the year, it frequents the coastal mud-flats and mangrove swamps, and the banks of all types of inland waterway. Not shy, it is usually seen alone or in small groups, preferring not to associate with other wading birds. It continually bobs its head and tail as it hurries along the mud-flats searching for crabs, small fishes, shrimps and aquatic insects. When flushed from its habitat, it usually gives a sudden piping alarm call, and then flies in a semicircle over the water, returning to continue feeding in the same place once more. The Spotted Sandpiper winters throughout the Caribbean and South America, as far south as Chile.

Spotted Sandpiper (*Actitis macularia*)

WADERS AND WATERBIRDS

Wattled Jacana   *Jacana jacana*

Local name: Spurwing
Family: Jacanas   Distribution

Wattled Jacana
(*Jacana jacana*)

The Jacana is common wherever there are canals, flooded rice fields or freshwater swamps. This graceful little bird can be observed in pairs or small flocks as it seems to walk magically on the surface of the water. In fact, its extraordinarily elongated toes spread its weight so successfully that it is able to move easily across water on the flimsiest of floating vegetation. Both the adults and the chicks can swim, and they often dive expertly to avoid danger. The Jacana aggressively defends its young, either by attacking the intruder noisily or by feigning injury to distract and lure the intruder away from the chicks. As the adult alights, it holds its lemon-coloured wings erect for a moment, exposing a spur on the bend of each wing (shown above). The Wattled Jacana spends its entire life near water, where it feeds on insects, small fish and all manner of aquatic life. Even its nest is on the water, and is usually composed of a few pieces of aquatic vegetation loosely arranged on the broad leaves of the water-lily plant. The Jacana ranges from Panama to as far south as Bolivia.

Black Skimmer

Rynchops niger

Family: Skimmers

Distribution

The Black Skimmer is a large gregarious bird with a scissors-like bill, which commonly frequents the coastal mud-flats, mangrove swamps and estuaries, as well as the rivers of the interior grasslands. This partially nocturnal bird has a bill that is specially adapted to its unique method of feeding. It flies very low, skimming the surface of the water with its open bill, in search of small fish, plankton or crustaceans. It sometimes nests in large colonies on open beaches or on the sandbanks of rivers. The range of the Black Skimmer extends from the southern USA, through most of South America, to the southern-most tip of Argentina.

Black Skimmer (*Rynchops niger*)

WADERS AND WATERBIRDS

Ringed Kingfisher   *Ceryle torquata*

Local name: Under Bridge
Family: Kingfishers   Distribution

A solitary bird, the Ringed Kingfisher is the largest of the four species of kingfisher found in Guyana. Its habitat includes mangroves and rice fields, but it is most commonly seen flying in front of boats travelling along Guyana's many rivers. As its name suggests, this bird is a master fisherman and dives headlong below the surface of the water to seize its prey, before flying back to its perch overlooking the river to devour it. Besides fish, it feeds on shrimps, frogs and insects, and it nests in the dry weather in a hole in the bank of the river. The Ringed Kingfisher ranges from Mexico through Central America and the Caribbean, as well as most of South America.

Ringed Kingfisher (*Ceryle torquata*)

4 Insect eaters

Lineated Woodpecker (*Dryocopus lineatus*)

Great Kiskadee

Pitangus sulphuratus

Local name: Kiskadee
Family: Tyrant Flycatchers

Distribution

This is undoubtedly one of Guyana's noisiest and best-known birds. It is common throughout the country, and is easily recognised by its 'kis-kis-ka-dee' call, which can be heard all day, even towards nightfall. The Kiskadee is usually found in pairs or small restless groups that often frequent residential areas. It also enjoys the proximity of water, and can sometimes be seen splashing into ponds and trenches in search of small fish. Its other food consists of lizards, palm seeds, peppers, fruits and – especially – insects, which are captured on the wing. The nest, a bulky untidy structure, is made of grass and other plant material. It is usually found high up in trees or on telephone poles, and after the necessary repairs may be used on more than one occasion. The Great Kiskadee is very aggressive when protecting its nest against hawks or other predators. It ranges from as far north as southern Texas, throughout South America, down to Argentina in the south.

Great Kiskadee (*Pitangus sulphuratus*)

Tropical Kingbird

Tyrannus melancholicus

Local name: Ball Catcher
Family: Tyrant Flycatchers

Distribution

Tropical Kingbird (*Tyrannus melancholius*)

Widespread throughout most regions of Guyana, the Tropical Kingbird is well known for the aggressive defence of its territory, and can be often seen attacking hawks and other birds, chasing them away. An excellent, sometimes acrobatic, flier, it can hover in the air to catch insects on the wing. Its nest is a shallow cup of sticks located among shrubs and low trees. The range of the Tropical Kingbird extends from Mexico in the north, through the countries of Central and South America, as far south as Argentina.

White-headed Marsh Tyrant *Arundinicola leucocephala*

Local name: Policeman
Family: Tyrant Flycatchers

Distribution

A small, shy bird, the White-headed Marsh Tyrant is not as common as the other species of tyrant found in Guyana. It is found in the marshlands and wet savannahs of the coast, as well as along the rivers of the interior. It is more often found in pairs in the low shrubs, where it feeds on butterflies, grasshoppers, dragonflies and other insects. Its small nest, lined with grass and feathers, is usually attached to the branches of trees overhanging the water. The range of the White-headed Marsh Tyrant includes Trinidad, Venezuela, Surinam, Brazil, Bolivia, Paraguay and Argentina.

White-headed Marsh Tyrant (*Arundinicola leucocephala*)

Pied Water-Tyrant *Fluvicola pica*

Local name: Cotton Strainer or Washer Woman
Family: Tyrant Flycatchers

Distribution

This attractive little bird, with its smart black-and-white plumage, is a common sight along the coastlands. It flits about in the vegetation on the banks of canals, trenches and other waterways, never straying far from water. The Pied Water-Tyrant is a conspicuous, active bird, often seen in residential areas, in pairs and small groups, always near the ground or on a branch overhanging the water. Steadily twitching its tail, it continuously scours the foliage for the insects and small seeds on which it feeds. The dome-shaped nest is constructed in the open, but usually attached to a small tree with the entrance close to the water. The Pied Water-Tyrant ranges from Panama in the north, to Trinidad and throughout most of South America.

Pied Water-Tyrant (*Fluvicola pica*)

INSECT EATERS

Vermilion Flycatcher *Pyrocephalus rubinus*

Family: Tyrant Flycatchers   Distribution

Unlike most of the small flycatchers, which are dull in colour, the plumage of the male Vermilion Flycatcher is unique in the family. The bird is found in the open country of the coastland and the interior savannahs, where it is known for its peculiar, aerial displays, with wings vibrating while it utters its low, sweet call. Its diet includes flies, crickets, grasshoppers and other insects. It aggressively defends its nest, which is a bowl-shaped construction placed in the fork of a low tree. The range of the Vermilion Flycatcher includes the USA, Nicaragua and most of South America, as far south as Chile.

Vermilion Flycatcher (*Pyrocephalus rubinus*)

38 BIRDS OF GUYANA

Fork-tailed Flycatcher — *Tyrannus savana*

Local name: Scissors Tail
Family: Tyrant Flycatchers

Distribution

A migrant species, the Fork-tailed Flycatcher occurs in almost all regions of Guyana, especially between March and October. It prefers the open country of the coastland and the interior savannahs, where it is sometimes seen in huge flocks of more than 100 birds. It is entirely insectivorous, and is usually seen on a high perch, opening and closing its elegant tail, as it waits to pounce on the butterflies, grasshoppers, dragonflies and other insects that make up its diet. Its nest is an untidy structure of grass and other plant fibres, in low trees or shrubs. The Fork-tailed Flycatcher has an extensive range, from Mexico in the north, and throughout South America, to as far south as the Falkland Islands.

Fork-tailed Flycatcher (*Tyrannus savana*)

INSECT EATERS

Southern House Wren
Troglodytes musculus

Local name: God Bird
Family: Wrens

Distribution

Few birds are as unmistakable and familiar as the House Wren. Not shy, it fearlessly enters houses, where it can be seen flitting around in search of spiders and insects. It is widespread in the coastal regions, inhabiting savannahs, plantations and gardens in residential areas, but not the deep forest. A busy bird, full of energy, it may often be seen in pairs, foraging in the bushes or on the ground between tree roots for insects and larvae. This bird is a fine whistler. Although small, it can be heard for quite a distance, and its sweet bubbling notes are a delight to the ear. The nest is an open cup-shaped structure of loosely arranged sticks, plant material and feathers. Nests can be found in the most peculiar places, such as old flowerpots, letterboxes and even inside houses, on shelves and beams. The Southern House Wren ranges from Mexico in the north, throughout the Caribbean and most of South America, to Argentina in the south.

Southern House Wren (*Troglodytes musculus*)

Pale-breasted Thrush
Turdus leucomelas

Family: Thrushes

Distribution

The Pale-breasted Thrush is a rather dull-coloured bird that is best known for its melodious song, which is heard well before dawn and continues after dusk. It is found throughout most of Guyana, and is one of the most common birds among centres of population. It is often seen hopping along the ground feeding on seeds, insects and especially worms, which it captures by stuffing its beak into the mud. It is fond of nesting in shrubs or under the floor beams of buildings, where it makes a nest lined with moss and grass roots. The Pale-breasted Thrush's range includes Surinam, Brazil, Peru, Paraguay and Bolivia, and stretches as far south as Argentina.

Pale-breasted Thrush (*Turdus leucomelas*)

Gray-breasted Martin *Progne chalybea*

Local name: Swallow
Family: Swallows

Distribution

The Gray-breasted Martin is one of the most common members of the swallow family. These sleek graceful birds are strong rapid fliers, showing great agility in the air. They can often be seen darting back and forth, diving at insects caught on the wing, which make up their main diet. Often seen in large flocks, sometimes mixed with other species of swallow, they perch on dry trees or in long lines on electric wires. When disturbed, they fly off to soar the skies for a while, only to alight on the same perch a short time later. The nest is an untidy collection of sticks and dry grass. Showing little fear of humans, these birds usually locate their nests in openings under house roofs on beams and rafters, or in natural hollows in rocks or even in termite nests. The Gray-breasted Martin ranges from Texas in the north through Mexico and Central America to Argentina in the south.

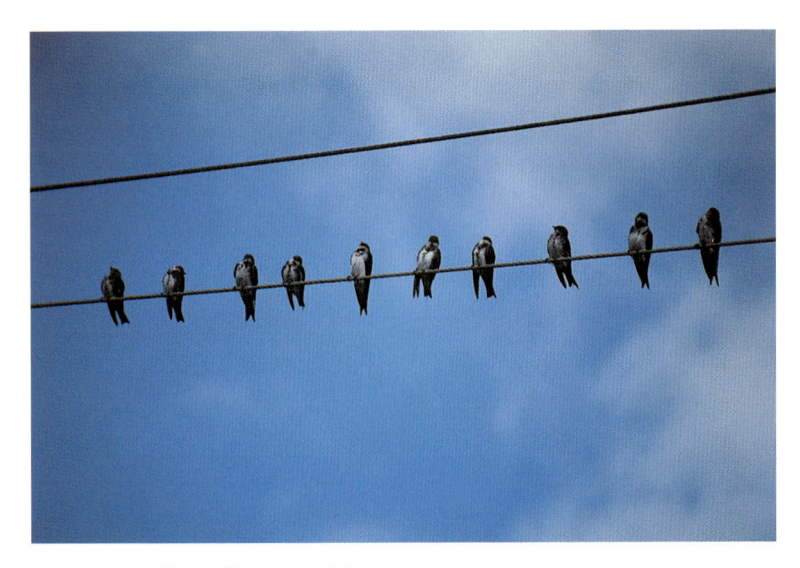

Gray-breasted Martin (*Progne chalybea*)

Smooth-billed Ani *Crotophaga ani*

Local name: Old Witch or Jumby Bird
Family: Cuckoos

Distribution

The Smooth-billed Ani is the smaller of the two species of Ani found in Guyana. It is an odd-looking, unattractive bird, with a large beak and strange call. Long ago it was regarded with some superstition, which resulted in its being given the sinister local names of 'Old Witch' or 'Jumby Bird'. It occurs throughout the pastures, gardens and grasslands of both the coast and interior in large, noisy flocks of up to 20 birds. Although its oversize tail makes it a clumsy flier, it is quite agile on the ground, where it is often seen close to grazing animals in order to feed on the lizards, grasshoppers and insects disturbed by them. Its bulky nest of dry twigs and leaves is usually made in low trees or thorn bushes. The Smooth-billed Ani ranges from South Florida and throughout the Caribbean to as far south as northern Argentina.

Smooth-billed Ani (*Crotophaga ani*)

INSECT EATERS *43*

Greater Ani
Crotophaga major

Local name: Jumbie Bird
Family: Cuckoos

Distribution

The Greater Ani is the largest of the three species of Ani found in Guyana. It is easily distinguished from the other two species by its iridescent plumage, large curved bill and prominent, white eyes. Not as gregarious as the other species, it is found in thick vegetation along the banks of both coastal and interior rivers. Its main diet consists of insects, but it also eats small fruit, frogs and lizards. Its nest is an untidy group of sticks, secluded in the tangled riverbank vegetation. The range of the Greater Ani extends from Panama in the north, through northern South America to Brazil and as far south as Argentina.

Greater Ani (*Crotophaga major*)

Paradise Jacamar   *Galbula dea*

Family: Jacamars   Distribution

The Paradise Jacamar is fairly common along forest trails and open woodlands, as well as in the more remote forests of the interior. It resembles an oversized hummingbird and is usually seen in pairs, high in trees at the edge of the forest, on the lookout for insects, which are its sole diet. It nests in a burrow or hole that it makes in the sandy clay of the bank of a river or sometimes in a termite nest, high in a tree. The range of the Paradise Jacamar includes Colombia, Venezuela, Surinam, Brazil, Ecuador, Peru and Bolivia.

Paradise Jacamar (*Galbula dea*)

INSECT EATERS

Lineated Woodpecker *Dryocopus lineatus*

Local name: Carpenter Bird
Family: Woodpeckers

Distribution

The unmistakable, loud drumming on a hollow tree echoing through the forest announces the presence of a woodpecker. This species is common throughout most of Guyana as its habitat ranges from the dense forests of the interior to the coconut plantations of the coastal regions, as well as the trees and lampposts of population centres. Its strong beak is used to chisel the bark on tree-trunks in order to locate the ants, beetles, termites, spiders, and larvae on which it feeds. Even its sharp claws are specially adapted so as to hold the bird in a vertical position while feeding and in its nest in the cavity of a hollow tree. The range of this fascinating bird includes the countries of Central and South America.

Lineated Woodpecker (*Dryocopus lineatus*)

46 BIRDS OF GUYANA

Tropical Mockingbird *Mimus gilvus*

Family: Mockingbirds and Thrushes   Distribution

The Tropical Mockingbird comes from a small family of birds that are noted for their melodious calls. It is fairly common in the coastal countryside, near dwellings, as well as in the savannahs of the interior. This bird can move quickly along the ground, and has the ability to imitate the calls of frogs and crickets, as well as those of other birds. It is aggressive in the defence of its feeding grounds, where it forages for the fruit, insects, frogs and lizards that make up its diet. It nests in a bulky open cup of sticks, lined with grass, leaves and pieces of string and well concealed in the low branches of trees. The range of the Tropical Mockingbird includes Mexico, parts of the Caribbean and Brazil.

Tropical Mockingbird (*Mimus gilvus*)

Black-capped Donacobius — *Donacobius atricapillus*

Local name: Cuckoo
Family: Wrens

Distribution

The Black-capped Donacobius is fairly common in the marshes, rice fields, water conservancies and palm swamps that make up its habitat. Usually seen in pairs, it forages in the low, thick foliage for fruit, insects and worms. Its nest, which it protects aggressively, is a medium-sized construction of plant material. The range of the Black-capped Donacobius includes Panama, Venezuela, Surinam, Brazil, Ecuador, Peru and Argentina.

Black-capped Donacobius (*Donacobius atricapillus*)

Gray-winged Trumpeter *Psophia crepitans*

Local name: Warakabra
Family: Trumpeters

Distribution

The Gray-winged Trumpeter is fairly common throughout the forests of Guyana. Terrestrial by nature, it is encountered in small flocks along forest trails, where it feeds on fallen fruits, worms, grubs and insects. As its name suggests, the Trumpeter makes a loud, booming, vibrating call when it is alarmed. This is accompanied by the raising of the back feathers and aggressive posturing, in an effort to appear fearsome. It nests in trees in natural cavities, which it lines with leaves. The range of the Gray-winged Trumpeter includes the northern countries of South America, as well as Brazil, Ecuador and Peru.

Gray-winged Trumpeter (*Psophia crepitans*)

INSECT EATERS

Glittering-throated Emerald — *Amazilia fimbriata*

Local name: Doctor Zwee
Family: Hummingbirds

Distribution

Glittering-throated Emerald (*Amazilia fimbriata*)

The hummingbird is one of the wonders of the bird world. It is amazing to see this lovely little creature moving through the air suspended, as if by magic, on humming wings. The Glittering-throated Emerald is widespread because it is equally at home in gardens, open spaces or forests, in fact wherever flowering plants are found. It is usually solitary, but may be seen in pairs, and it shows a complete disregard for the presence of human beings. A specialised feeder, the hummingbird uses its long needle-like bill to extract nectar as it hovers in front of flowers. It also feeds on tiny soft insects caught while probing these blooms. This interesting bird establishes territories that it defends vigorously against all intruders, even members of its own family. The nest is a delicate cup-shaped structure of cotton, feathers, moss and other plant material. The Glittering-throated Emerald ranges through South America as far south as Bolivia and Paraguay.

Blue-chinned Sapphire *Chlorestes notatus*

Family: Hummingbirds   Distribution

Hummingbirds are a large family of small, colourful birds found only in the Western Hemisphere. The Blue-chinned Sapphire, with its striking, iridescent plumage, can be seen near forest edges and along the banks of rivers in the interior, feeding on the brightly coloured flowers that abound in this habitat. It also uses its incredible speed and acrobatic flying skills to capture mosquitoes, spiders and other small insects, which provide protein in its diet. It defends its territory aggressively, attacking much larger birds than itself. The hummingbird's nest is a miniature work of art, usually consisting of a small cup of plant material lined with feathers and decorated with lichen. The range of the Blue-chinned Sapphire includes Colombia, Venezuela, Trinidad, Surinam, Brazil and Peru.

Blue-chinned Sapphire (*Chlorestes notatus*)

INSECT EATERS

5 Grain and seed eaters

Grassland Yellow-Finch (*Sicalis luteola*)

Blue-black Grassquit *Volatinia jacarina*

Local name: Pee-Zing
Family: Finches

Distribution

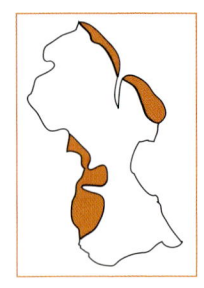

The Blue-black Grassquit is a very common bird that is found throughout the open country of the coastlands and along the forest edges, where it is usually seen in pairs or in small flocks. The shiny, black plumage of the male is especially conspicuous when it performs its unique aerial display. Jumping upwards from its perch, about 0.6 m (2 feet) in the air, it utters a high pitched 'Pee-Zing' call and then with a downward half-somersault lands on its perch again. Its diet consists of grass seeds, paddy and other grain. The nest of the Blue-black Grassquit is a small cup-shaped structure found in the low shrubs or on the ground. Its range extends from Mexico, through Central America, Trinidad, Colombia, Venezuela, Surinam and Brazil, as far south as Bolivia.

Blue-black Grassquit (*Volatinia jacarina*)

Grassland Yellow-Finch *Sicalis luteola*

Local name: Canary
Family: Finches

Distribution

The Grassland Yellow-Finch is a fairly common bird in the open countryside of the coastlands and the savannahs of the interior. It forages in pairs or small groups in the low shrubs for the grass and weed seeds that are its main diet. It is often kept as a pet because of its whistling ability. The nest of the Grassland Yellow-Finch is a shallow, cup-shaped structure found on the ground or in low vegetation. The bird ranges from Mexico and Panama in the north, through to most of the countries of South America.

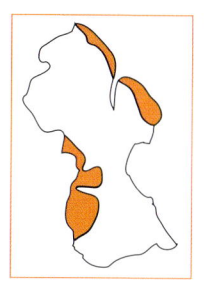

Grassland Yellow-Finch (*Sicalis luteola*)

GRAIN AND SEED EATERS

Red-capped Cardinal

Paroaria gularis

Local name: Red Head
Family: Finches

Distribution

The Red-capped Cardinal is one of the most attractive birds seen in the coastlands. It has a wide range of habitats including mangrove and courida forests, farms, pastures and residential areas. It is usually seen in pairs or small groups foraging among the shrubs and bushes for insects, seeds and fruits. It is always attached to a definite area, and guards this territory fiercely against intruding birds. Not shy, it can easily be attracted to feeding stations and bird baths. The nest is an open cup-shaped structure, usually found in the shrubbery along rivers or canals. The Red-capped Cardinal ranges throughout the northern countries of South America as far south as Bolivia.

Red-capped Cardinal (*Paroaria gularis*)

Yellow-hooded Blackbird *Agelaius icterocephalus*

Family: New World Blackbirds Distribution

The Yellow-hooded Blackbird is a handsome, gregarious bird that is often seen in large flocks in marshlands, rice fields and water conservancies of the coastland. They are particularly prevalent in rice fields, where they cause some crop damage as they forage for paddy and insects that are their main diet. The Yellow-hooded Blackbird nests in colonies, near the ground between reeds and other thick marsh vegetation. It is found in Trinidad, Colombia, Venezuela, Surinam and Peru.

Yellow-hooded Blackbird (*Agelaius icterocephalus*)

GRAIN AND SEED EATERS

Red-breasted Blackbird — *Sturnella militaris*

Local name: Robin Red Breast
Family: New World Blackbirds

Distribution

Despite its local name, this bird is not a robin at all but a member of the blackbird family. It is quite common in the pastures, wet grasslands and rice fields of the coast, but it also occurs inland to the mountains. It can be seen in small flocks continuously on the move, searching in the grass for its food, which consists of insects, grain, seeds and small fruits. It even eats small water creatures. The striking red-and-black plumage of the male is in sharp contrast to the dull brown colouring of the female, which serves as an effective camouflage in the grass. The male, by contrast, perches conspicuously on small bushes or fence posts. It has a peculiar habit of suddenly flying straight up about 6 m (20 feet) in the air, uttering a shrill cry, then diving quickly down to perch in the same place once more. The Red-breasted Blackbird ranges from Central America and the Caribbean in the north to as far south as Peru and Brazil.

Red-breasted Blackbird (*Sturnella militaris*)

Carib Grackle

Quiscalus lugubris

Local name: Corn Bird
Family: New World Blackbirds

Distribution

The male of this gregarious species is easily recognised by its glossy black iridescent plumage and yellow eyes. It has a peculiar wedge-shaped tail, which is often folded together upward in flight, hence its common name 'Boat-Tail'. Not found in the forests, this bird is widespread throughout the pastures, rice fields and residential areas of the coastlands. Although it forages among the branches of trees for insects, seeds and fruit, it prefers paddy whenever it is available. Large flocks can be seen feeding wherever paddy is laid out to dry. Like the Egret, this bird occasionally follows grazing animals to feed on the ticks and other insects that are found there. Nesting in flocks in shrubbery and low bushes, this bird plasters its nest with mud before lining it with plant material. The Carib Grackle ranges throughout the Caribbean and the countries of northern South America.

Carib Grackle (*Quiscalus lugubris*)

GRAIN AND SEED EATERS

Shiny Cowbird

Molothrus bonariensis

Local name: Oatsie
Family: New World Blackbirds

Distribution

The Shiny Cowbird is a gregarious species commonly found in large, noisy flocks, in coastal mangroves, pastures and rice fields, and along forest edges. Its diet consists of fruit, worms and insects, but it is particularly fond of paddy, and is often seen feeding in the fields or on the drying areas. A nesting parasite, it lays its eggs in the nests of other birds, especially the House Wren. This results in the strange sight of the Wren caring for nestlings twice its own size, much to the detriment of its own young. The Shiny Cowbird is found in Panama, Venezuela, Trinidad, Surinam and Argentina, and as far south as Chile.

Shiny Cowbird (*Molothrus bonariensis*)

Pale-vented Pigeon *Columba cayennensis*

Family: Doves

Distribution

The Pale-vented Pigeon is the largest member of the dove family in Guyana. A common bird, it is found in coastal plantations, in rice fields, and in forest along the banks of rivers. It occurs in pairs or sometimes in seasonal flocks of several hundred birds. A menace to rice farmers, it is hunted for its meat. Its main diet consists of berries, seeds and paddy. Its nest is a collection of small sticks lined with feathers, and is usually found in the upper branches of trees. The Pale-vented Pigeon ranges from Mexico though Central America, Colombia, Venezuela, Trinidad, Surinam and Brazil to as far south as Argentina.

Pale-vented Pigeon (*Columba cayennensis*)

GRAIN AND SEED EATERS

Ruddy Ground-Dove

Columbina talpacoti

Local name: Dove
Family: Doves

Distribution

Of the three species of ground-dove found in Guyana, the Ruddy Ground-Dove is the best known. The male of the species, with its blue-grey head and reddish-brown plumage, differs from the female, which is a uniformly dull brown in colour. It is largely terrestrial or ground dwelling, and can be seen moving busily along in search of seeds, paddy or other grain. It is common throughout the coastland and the open country and savannahs of the interior. A strong flier, when disturbed it takes wing with a sudden loud fluttering sound, usually from close under foot. The nest is a simple construction of grass and twigs located in low bushes in pastures or in small trees in residential areas. The Ruddy Ground-Dove ranges from as far north as Mexico, through Central America, the Caribbean and South America down to Argentina in the south.

Ruddy Ground-Dove (*Columbina talpacoti*)

Crested Bobwhite

Colinus cristatus

Local name: Savannah Quail
Family: Quails

Distribution

The Crested Bobwhite, a member of the quail family, is a gregarious species. This shy, elusive bird is fairly common in the open forests and savannahs of the interior. Almost exclusively terrestrial, it is so well camouflaged that it remains still until almost trodden upon, before erupting into flight with a loud beating of wings. It forages in the grass or undergrowth of its habitat for fallen fruit, worms, insects, seeds and grass. The nest is a shallow depression in the ground lined with dry leaves and grass. The Bobwhite's range includes Colombia, Venezuela, Surinam and Brazil.

Crested Bobwhite (*Colinus cristatus*)

GRAIN AND SEED EATERS *63*

6 Fruit eaters

Blue and Yellow Macaw (*Ara ararauna*)

Little Chachalaca
Ortalis motmot

Local name: Hannaqua
Family: Curassows and Guans

Distribution

The Little Chachalaca is widespread throughout the forests and savannahs of the interior. It has a loud, unique call heard mainly at dawn and dusk, which usually betrays its presence. Not a strong flier, it inhabits the thick foliage along forest edges, where it is very agile jumping from branch to branch, while feeding on flowers and fruits in the treetops. It also forages on the ground for seeds, insects, frogs and lizards. Its nest is a loose collection of twigs, low in the branches of a tree. The range of the Little Chachalaca includes Surinam, Venezuela and Brazil.

Little Chachalaca (*Ortalis motmot*)

Spix's Guan
Penelope jacquacu

Local name: Marudi
Family: Curassows and Guans

Distribution

This Guan is a shy bird that is often encountered in pairs or small groups, at dawn or in the late afternoon. Its meat is considered tasty, but though it is hunted in some areas, its dark colour makes it hard to see in the forest. It is fairly common in the upper reaches of the coastal and interior rivers, as well as in the more remote forests and savannahs. Its diet includes fallen fruit, insects, lizards, frogs and young leaves. The nest of the Spix's Guan is a loose construction of twigs in trees, usually not far from the ground. The bird is found in the countries of northern South America, as far south as Brazil and Bolivia.

Spix's Guan (*Penelope jacquacu*)

FRUIT EATERS 67

Black Curassow

Crax alector

Local name: Powis
Family: Curassows and Guans

Distribution

The Curassow is a fairly common bird, the size of a turkey, that inhabits the inland forests and savannah regions of Guyana. Usually encountered in pairs or small family groups, it is used as a source of meat by the inhabitants of interior settlements. It forages on the forest floor for fallen fruit, nuts, seeds, insects and small reptiles. Its nest is a platform of sticks placed in low trees or on the ground. The range of the Black Curassow includes Colombia, Venezuela, Surinam and Brazil.

Black Curassow (*Crax alector*)

Yellow-rumped Cacique

Cacicus cela

Local name: Mockingbird
Family: New World Blackbirds

Distribution

The musical, gurgling sounds of the Yellow-rumped Cacique can be heard from a great distance before the bird is actually seen. Besides a wide range of calls of its own, this noisy bird can also expertly imitate the calls of many other birds. Common throughout Guyana, it lives by forest edges, on the banks of rivers, and near centres of population. Its diet consists of fruit, berries, seeds and insects. Like the other members of the family, this Cacique is gregarious and nests in colonies by occupying a tall tree with dozens of large, oblong nests of plant fibres. The range of this fascinating bird includes Panama, Venezuela, Surinam, Brazil, Ecuador, Peru and Bolivia.

Yellow-rumped Cacique (*Cacicus cela*)

FRUIT EATERS

Crested Oropendola
Psarocolius decumanus

Local name: Bunya
Family: New World Blackbirds

Distribution

The Crested Oropendola is the largest of the four species of Cacique found in Guyana. It is a fairly common bird that is found in the coconut estates of the coast, as well as the forests and savannahs of the interior. An active bird, it busily flies about the forest feeding on fruits, berries and seeds. It is found in large flocks in tall trees, where it performs unique, noisy displays involving the flapping of wings and a series of gurgling, musical notes. This bird breeds in colonies, with its beautifully woven, bag-like, hanging nests suspended from the ends of branches. The range of the Crested Oropendola includes Panama, Colombia, Venezuela, Trinidad and Brazil, and stretches as far south as Argentina.

Crested Oropendola (*Psarocolius decumanus*)

Yellow Oriole
Icterus nigrogularis

Local name: Yellow Plaintain
Family: New World Blackbirds

Distribution

The Yellow Oriole is one of the most beautiful birds commonly seen in the coastlands. It is usually seen in pairs; the plumage of the male is brighter than that of the female. The bird inhabits banana plantations, coastal mangroves, pastures and gardens, wherever ripe fruit may be found. It is a pleasant sight to see as it flits from branch to branch in search of insects and caterpillars that are also a source of food. If feeding together on a ripe fruit, the other fruit eaters such as the Tanagers retreat when the Yellow Oriole approaches. The nest is an elongated, almost bottle-shaped construction that is usually attached to the end of a small branch, sometimes over water. The Yellow Oriole is found in Trinidad, and the islands off Venezuela, as well as the northern countries of South America.

Yellow Oriole (*Icterus nigrogularis*)

FRUIT EATERS

Blue-gray Tanager — *Thraupis episcopus*

Local name: Blue Sackie
Family: Tanagers

Distribution

The Blue-gray Tanager is the best-known member of the tanager or sackie family as they are known locally. It is a pleasure to observe this beautiful silvery-blue bird as it restlessly flits through the treetops, uttering a series of high-pitched calls. This conspicuous bird is distributed throughout Guyana, where it inhabits many different types of vegetation. It frequents residential areas, where it can be seen in pairs or small groups feeding on ripe fruits and insects. Not shy, it can readily be attracted to feeding trays with bananas, mangoes or other fruits. The nest is a construction of grass and leaves often made in trees close to houses. The Blue-gray Tanager sometimes takes over the nest of a smaller bird, and when the eggs are hatched it feeds its own young along with those of the ejected builder. It ranges from Southern Mexico and the Caribbean to as far south as Bolivia.

Blue-gray Tanager (*Thraupis episcopus*)

Palm Tanager
Thraupis palmarum

Local name: Coconut Saki
Family: Tanagers

Distribution

Like the other species of tanager, the Palm Tanager is common throughout most of Guyana. It is a busy bird, whose call can be heard as it flits from tree to tree in search of fruit, caterpillars, termites and other insects. Its nest is a cup-shaped structure of grass and leaves, usually high up in trees. The Palm Tanager is found in Trinidad, Brazil, Ecuador, Peru, Paraguay and Bolivia.

Palm Tanager (*Thraupis palmarum*)

FRUIT EATERS

Violaceous Euphonia *Euphonia violacea*

Local name: Plantain Canary
Family: Tanagers

Distribution

The Violaceous Euphonia is a small, colourful bird that is fairly common in coastal plantations and around human dwellings, as well as in the forests of the interior. Usually seen in small groups, it feeds on ripe fruit, seeds and insects, and is often kept as a pet because of its melodious whistle. It prefers nesting near houses, in gardens or in thick shrubbery, where it constructs a dome-shaped nest of fine plant material. Its range includes Trinidad, Surinam, Venezuela and Brazil, and stretches as far south as Argentina.

Violaceous Euphonia (*Euphonia violacea*)

Red-fan Parrot — *Deroptyus accipitrinus*

Local name: Hawk-headed Parrot
Family: Parrots

Distribution

Red-fan Parrot
(*Deroptyus accipitrinus*)

With its crimson crest edged with blue, the Red-fan Parrot is both remarkable and different from the other species of parrot in Guyana. Even in flight this parrot looks quite different. With its rounded tail and screeching cry, it resembles a hawk more than it does a parrot. Usually seen in pairs and not in flocks, this uncommon bird inhabits the coastal rivers, inland forest and mountain regions. It feeds on fruits, nuts and seeds, and nests in holes in the trunks of trees. When angry or agitated this bird raises its beautiful neck feathers to form a sort of fan at the back of its head. This device is used to intimidate intruders. Although the bird can be tamed, it does not talk easily. The Red-fan Parrot has a very limited range, which includes only the northern countries of South America.

Yellow-crowned Parrot — *Amazona ochrocephala*

Local name: White-eyed Amazon Parrot
Family: Parrots

Distribution

Yellow-crowned Parrot (*Amazona ochrocephala*)

The Yellow-crowned Parrot is one of the largest and least noisy of the many species of parrot to be found in Guyana. Not often seen in coastal areas, it is widespread and abundant in the forests, and inland to the mountain regions. In the early morning, and again at dusk, numerous pairs can be seen flying with rapid wing beats over the forest canopy, calling all the time. Its food consists of ripe fruits, nuts and seeds, and it does considerable damage in cultivated plots. The Yellow-crowned Parrot is found in Ecuador, Peru, Brazil and Mexico.

Orange-winged Parrot
Amazona amazonica

Local name: Screecher
Family: Parrots

Distribution

Orange-winged Parrot (*Amazona amazonica*)

The Orange-winged Parrot is the most common and one of the noisiest parrots in Guyana. Widespread in the forests and savannahs of all regions, large flocks of more than 100 birds can be often seen overhead in the late afternoon as they return to their roosts. Considered a pest in cultivated areas because of its damage to crops, it feeds on mangoes, oranges, berries and blossoms. It usually nests in a hole in the trunk of a palm tree. The Orange-winged Parrot is found in the northern countries of South America as well as in Brazil, Peru and Ecuador.

FRUIT EATERS

Blue-headed Parrot
Pionus menstruus

Family: Parrots

Distribution

The Blue-headed Parrot is widespread throughout the forests of coastal and inland rivers, as well as the more remote mountain forests of the interior. It is usually found in small flocks foraging for ripe fruits, seeds, nuts and insects, and has been known to cause damage to crops. Besides its blue head, this parrot can be distinguished from other species by its high-pitched screeching call, but it nests in a hole in the trunk of a tree, like other members of the parrot family. Its range includes the countries of northern South America, as far south as Bolivia.

Blue-headed Parrot (*Pionus menstrusus*)

Black-headed Parrot *Pionites melanocephala*

Local name: Seven Colour Parrot
Family: Parrots

Distribution

Black-headed Parrot (*Pionites melanocephala*)

The Black-headed Parrot is fairly common, especially in the forests of north-western Guyana. It is also found in forest edges along the coast and water conservancies, where it occurs in noisy flocks feeding in the treetops. Its diet includes fruits, berries, seeds and nuts, and it nests in an unlined hole in the trunk of a tree. The range of the Black-headed Parrot includes Colombia, Venezuela, Surinam, Brazil and Peru.

FRUIT EATERS

Red-bellied Macaw — *Ara manilata*

Local name: Ite Macaw
Family: Parrots

Distribution

Red-bellied Macaw (*Ara manilata*)

One of the two smaller species of macaw found in Guyana, the Red-bellied Macaw is by far the most common. It is found in small flocks in the palm swamps, water conservancies and cultivated areas of the coast, as well as in the forests and savannahs of the interior. Although it feeds on other fruit, seeds and nuts, the fruit of the Ite Palm is the main item of its diet. It nests in holes in the trunks of palm trees, usually in a swamp to provide added protection from predators. The range of the Red-bellied Macaw includes Trinidad, Colombia, Venezuela, Surinam, Brazil, Peru, Ecuador and Bolivia.

Blue and Yellow Macaw
Ara ararauna

Family: Parrots   Distribution

Blue and Yellow Macaw (*Ara ararauna*)

The Blue and Yellow Macaw is the most common of the five species of macaw that are recorded in Guyana. This handsome bird is more numerous and widespread than the other species, and is found in the forest along both the coastal and interior rivers. It also frequents the savannahs and palm forests inland to the mountains. It is a rather sluggish bird that can be seen in large flocks of 20 or more feeding noisily in the tree tops on the abundance of ripe fruits, seeds and nuts to be found there. The Macaw's loud harsh call is often heard as it flies over the jungle canopy, especially in the early morning and just before dusk. It usually nests in holes in the trunks of the highest palm trees. It is easily tamed, making an interesting pet. The Blue and Yellow Macaw is also found in Central and South America, ranging from Panama in the north to Bolivia in the south.

FRUIT EATERS *81*

Red and Green Macaw — *Ara chloroptera*

Local name: Big Head
Family: Parrots

Distribution

Red and Green Macaw (*Ara chloroptera*)

The Red and Green Macaw is one of the three large species of macaw that are found in Guyana. Fairly common in the mountain and lowland forests of the upper reaches rivers, this noisy bird can be usually seen in pairs or small groups flying over the forest canopy. It feeds in the treetops on fruits and nuts, and uses its massive beak to crack the seeds of various palms. Like the other species of the parrot family, it nests in holes in the trunks of trees. The range of this beautiful bird includes Panama, Colombia, Venezuela, Surinam Brazil and Bolivia.

Scarlet Macaw   *Ara macao*

Family: Parrots

Distribution

Scarlet Macaw (*Ara macao*)

The Scarlet Macaw is surely one of the most spectacular and brilliantly coloured birds in the world. This is the largest of our macaws, and is fairly common throughout the forests of the interior, especially along inland rivers. It also occurs in savannah areas, and it frequents cultivated fields, where it supplements its usual diet of fruits with corn, resulting in its being considered a pest by farmers. Unlike the Blue and Yellow Macaw it is usually seen in pairs or small flocks, or even as a solitary bird. The nest generally consists of a hole in a dead tree. If this is too small the bird enlarges it with its strong beak. Like the other species of macaw, the Scarlet is easily tamed and is a popular if noisy pet. It ranges from Mexico in the north, through Central and South America as far south as Bolivia and Paraguay.

FRUIT EATERS

Black-necked Aracari — *Pteroglossus aracari*

Local name: Toucanet
Family: Toucans

Distribution

The Black-necked Aracari is one of the most common species of the toucan family represented in Guyana. It is widespread in the coastal plantations as well as in the savannahs and forests of the interior. Usually seen in small flocks, it feeds on soft fruit, berries, lizards, insects and birds' eggs. Like the other members of this family, it nests in holes in the trunks of tall trees. The Black-necked Aracari ranges throughout Venezuela, Surinam and Brazil.

Black-necked Aracari (*Pteroglossus aracari*)

Channel-billed Toucan   *Ramphastos vitellinus*

Local name: Bill Bird
Family: Toucans

Distribution

Channel-billed Toucan (*Ramphastos vitellinus*)

The Channel-billed Toucan is less colourful than the other large species of toucan that inhabit Guyana. It is common throughout the interior forests and the upper reaches of both coastal and inland rivers. It is usually seen in small flocks high in the treetops feeding on fruit, berries, nuts, seeds, and the eggs and nestlings of other birds. The Channel-billed Toucan nests in holes or natural cavities in the trunks of trees, and is also found in Trinidad and the northern countries of South America, as far south as Brazil.

Red-billed Toucan

Ramphastos tucanus

Local name: Bill Bird
Family: Toucans

Distribution

Of the five large species of toucan in Guyana the Red-billed Toucan is the best known. It is common and widespread throughout the forests of the interior. Not particularly shy, it is an active, noisy and inquisitive bird. It has a habit of sitting on the topmost branches of trees and uttering loud bugling notes at regular intervals, jerking its tail and throwing its bill in the air. It is regarded by the Amerindians as a sure weatherman, as it usually calls loudly just before the rain falls. Seen in pairs and occasionally in small groups, it feeds mostly on ripe fruits, berries, seeds and insects. In spite of its unbalanced appearance its flight is easy and swift, and it nests in the hollow trunks of tall trees about 10 m (30 feet) from the ground. Easily kept in captivity, it makes a noisy but inquisitive pet. The Red-billed Toucan ranges throughout South America as far as northern Argentina.

Red-billed Toucan (*Ramphastos tucanus*)

Toco Toucan

Ramphastos toco

Local name: Bill Bird
Family: Toucans

Distribution

The Toco Toucan is one of the most beautiful species of toucan. Its tremendous bill, among the most remarkable in the bird world, is almost as large as the rest of its body. It is found in coconut plantations, conservancies and coastal rivers, as well as in the forests of the interior and in mountain regions. It is an active, noisy bird, and is usually encountered in small groups foraging restlessly in the treetops. It feeds mainly on ripe fruits and berries, but will occasionally capture and eat small birds and lizards, as well as eggs. It has a graceful undulating flight, but it seldom flies long distances. The nest is located in holes and natural hollows in high trees in the forest. The Toco Toucan can be tamed easily, and is therefore a popular – if noisy – pet. It ranges from the Guianas through South America to northern Argentina.

Toco Toucan (*Ramphastos toco*)

FRUIT EATERS

Index

Note: page numbers in *italics* refer to illustrations separated from the text

Common names
Ani
   Greater 44
   Smooth-billed 43
Aracari, Black-necked 84

Ball Catcher 35
Baridi Hawk 10
Bat Falcon 10
Big Head 82
Bill Bird 85, 86, 87
Blackbirds
   Red-breasted 58
   Yellow-hooded 57
Black-capped Donacobius 48
Black-crowned Night Heron 21
Black Curassow 68
Black-headed Parrot 79
Black-necked Aracari 84
Black Skimmer 31
Black Vulture 13
Blue and Yellow Macaw *65*, 81
Blue-black Grassquit 54
Blue-chinned Sapphire 51
Blue-gray Tanager 72
Blue-headed Parrot 78
Blue Sackie 72
Boat-billed Heron 22
Bunya 70

Cacique 70
   Yellow-rumped 69
Canaries x
Canary (local name) 55
   Plantain 74
Canje Pheasant 2
Carib Grackle 59
Carpenter Bird 46
Carrion Crow 13
Cattle Egret 16
Channel-billed Toucan 85
Chicken Hawk 6, 7
Chow 19

Cocoi Heron 18
Coconut Saki 73
Corn Bird 59
Cotton Strainer 37
Cranes
   Honorora 18
   White 17
Crapaud Quack 22
Crested Bobwhite 63
Crested Caracara 5
Crested Oropendola 70
Cuckoo (local name) 48
Cuckoos
   Greater Ani 44
   Smooth-billed Ani 43
Curassows 66, 67
   Black 68

Doctor Zwee 50
Donacobius, Black-capped 48
Doves
   Pale-vented Pigeon 61
   Ruddy Ground 62
Ducks, Whistling xi, 28

Eagles viii
   Harpy Eagle xi, 4
Egrets ix
   Cattle 16
   Great 17
   White 16

Finches
   Blue-black Grassquit 54
   Grassland Yellow *53*, 55
   Red-capped Cardinal 56
Flycatchers: see Tyrant Flycatchers
Fork-tailed Flycatcher 39

Gauling 16, 20
Glittering-throated Emerald 50
God Bird 40

Grassland Yellow-Finch *53*, 55
Gray-breasted Martin 42
Gray-winged Trumpeter 49
Great Egret 17
Great Horned Owl 12
Great Kiskadee 34
Greater Ani 44
Guans
   Little Chachalaca 66
   Spix's 67

Hannaqua 66
Harpy Eagle xi, 4
Hawk-Eagle
   Black and White 9
   Ornate 8
Hawk-headed Parrot 75
Hawks xiii
   Baridi 10
   Kreketty 6
   White-tailed 7
Heeri 24
Herons ix
   Boat-billed 22
   Cocoi 18
   Rufescent Tiger-Heron 23
   Striated 19
   Tricolored *15*, 20
Hoatzin viii, *1*, 2
Honorara Crane 18
House Wren 60
Hummingbirds xi
   Blue-chinned Sapphire 51
   Glittering-throated Emerald 50

Ite Macaw 80

Jabiru Stork 25
Jacamar, Paradise 45
Jacana, Wattled xii, 30
Jumbie Bird 44
Jumby Bird 43

88 BIRDS OF GUYANA

Karow 26
King Vulture *3*, 14
Kingfisher, Ringed 32
Kiskadees ix
  Great 34
Kreketty Hawk 6

Limpkin 26
Lineated Woodpecker *33*, 46
Little Chachalaca 66

Macaws viii, xi
  Blue and Yellow *65*, 81
  Ite 80
  Red and Green 82
  Red-bellied 80
  Scarlet 83
  Seven Colour 79
Maguari Stork 24
Martin, Gray-breasted 42
Marudi 67
Mockingbird, Tropical 47
Mockingbird (local name) 69

Negrocop 25
New World Blackbirds
  Carib Grackle 59
  Crested Oropendola 70
  Red-breasted Blackbird 58
  Shiny Cowbird 60
  Yellow-hooded Blackbird 57
  Yellow Oriole 71
  Yellow-rumped Cacique 69
Night Herons xii, *xiii*
  Black-crowned 21

Oatsie 60
Old Witch 43
Orange-winged Parrot 77
Orioles x
  Yellow 71
Owls viii
  Great Horned 12
  Spectacled 11

Pale-breasted Thrush 41
Pale-vented Pigeon 61
Palm Tanager 73
Paradise Jacamar 45
Parrots viii, xi, xiii
  Black-headed 79
  Blue-headed 78
  Orange-winged 77
  Red-fan 75
  White-eyed Amazon 76

Yellow-crowned 76
  see also Macaws
Pee-Zing 54
Pied Water-Tyrant 37
Pigeon, Pale-vented 61
Plantain Canary 74
Plovers vii
  Southern Lapwing 27
Policeman 36
Powis 68
Quack 21
  Crapaud 22
Quails
  Crested Bobwhite 63
  Savannah 63

Red and Green Macaw 82
Red-bellied Macaw 80
Red-billed Toucan 86
Red-breasted Blackbird 58
Red-capped Cardinal 56
Red-fan Parrot 75
Red Head 56
Ringed Kingfisher 32
Robin Red Breast 58
Ruddy Ground Dove 62
Rufescent Tiger-Heron 23

Sandpipers ix
  Spotted 29
Savannah Quail 63
Scarlet Macaw 83
Scissors Tail 39
Screecher 77
Seven Colour Parrot 79
Shakey 29
Shiny Cowbird 60
Skimmer, Black 31
Smooth-billed Ani 43
Snail Kite 6
Southern House Wren 40
Southern Lapwing 27
Spectacled Owl 11
Spix's Guan 67
Spotted Sandpiper 29
Spurwing 30
Storks
  Jabiru 25
  Maguari 24
Striated Heron 19
Swallows ix, 42

Tanagers x, 71
  Blue-gray 72
  Palm 73
Violaceous Euphonia 74
Thrush, Pale-breasted 41
Tiger Bird 23

Tinamou xii
Toco Toucan 87
Toucanet 84
Toucans x
  Black-necked Aracari 84
  Channel-billed 85
  Red-billed 86
  Toco 87
Towa-Towas x
Tricolored Heron *15*, 20
Tropical Kingbird 35
Tropical Mockingbird 47
Trumpeter, Gray-winged 49
Tyrant Flycatchers
  Fork-tailed Flycatcher 39
  Kiskadee 34
  Pied Water-Tyrant 37
  Tropical Kingbird 35
  Vermilion Flycatcher 38
  White-headed Marsh Tyrant 36

Under Bridge 32

Vermilion Flycatcher 38
Violaceous Euphonia 74
Vultures viii, xi
  Black 13
  King *3*, 14

Warakabra 49
Washer Woman 37
Wattled Jacana xii, 30
Whistling-Ducks
  Black-bellied xi, 28
  White-faced 28
White Crane 17
White Egret 16
White-eyed Amazon Parrot 76
White-headed Marsh Tyrant 36
Wissy-Wissy 28
Woodpecker, Lineated *33*, 46
Wrens ix
  Black-capped Donacobius 48
  House 60
  Southern House 40

Yellow-crowned Parrot 76
Yellow-hooded Blackbird 57
Yellow Oriole 71
Yellow Plantain 71
Yellow-rumped Cacique 69

INDEX *89*

Scientific names

Actitis macularia 29
Agelaius icterocephalus 57
Amazilia fimbriata 50
Amazona amazonica 77
   ochrocephala 76
Ara ararauna 65, 81
   chloroptera 82
   macao 83
   manilata 80
Aramus guarauna 26
Ardea alba 17
   cocoi 18
Arundinicola leucocephala 36

Bubo virginianus 12
Bubulcus ibis 16
Buteo albicaudatus 7
Butorides striatus 19

Cacicus cela 69
Carcara cheriway 5
Ceryle torquata 32
Chlorestes notatus 51
Cochlearius cochlearius 22
Colinus cristatus 63
Columba cayennensis 61
Columbina talpacoti 62
Coragyps atratus 13
Crax alector 68
Crotophaga ani 43
   major 44

Dendrocygna autumnalis 28
   viduata 28
Deroptyus accipitrinus 75
Donacobius atricapillus 48
Dryocopus lineatus 33, 46

Egretta tricolor 15, 20
Euphonia violacea 74
Euxenura maguari 24

Falco rufigularis 10
Fluvicola pica 37

Galbula dea 45

Harpia harpyja 4

Icterus nigrogularis 71

Jabiru mycteria 25
Jacana jacana 30

Mimus gilvus 47
Molothrus bonariensis 60

Nycticorax nycticorax 21

Opisthocomus hoazin 1, 2
Ortalis motmot 66

Paroaria gularis 56
Penelope jacquacu 67
Pionites melanocephala 79

Pionus menstruus 78
Pitangus sulphuratus 34
Progne chalybea 42
Psarocolius decumanus 70
Psophia crepitans 49
Pteroglossus aracari 84
Pulsatrix perspicillata 11
Pyrocephalus rubinus 38

Quiscalus lugubris 59

Ramphastos toco 87
   tucanus 86
   vitellinus 85
Rostrhamus sociabilis 6
Rynchops niger 31

Sarcoramphus papa 3, 14
Sicalis luteola 53, 55
Spizaetus ornatus 8
Spizastur melanoleucus 9
Sturnella militaris 58

Thraupis episcopus 72
   palmarum 73
Tigrisoma lineatum 23
Troglodytes musculus 40
Turdus leucomelas 41
Tyrannus melancholicus 35
   savana 39

Vanellus chilensis 27
Volatinia jacarina 54